How to Sparkle at
PHONICS

Jo Laurence

 Brilliant Publications

We hope you and your class enjoy using this book. Other books in the series include:

English titles
How to Sparkle at Alphabet Skills	1 897675 17 8
How to Sparkle at Nursery Rhymes	1 897675 16 X
How to Sparkle at Prediction Skills	1 897675 15 1
How to Sparkle at Writing Stories and Poems	1 897675 18 6
How to Sparkle at Grammar and Punctuation	1 897675 19 4

Maths titles
How to Sparkle at Counting to 10	1 897675 27 5
How to Sparkle at Addition and Subtraction to 20	1 897675 28 3
How to Sparkle at Number Bonds	1 897675 34 8
How to Sparkle at Beginning Multiplication and Division	1 897675 30 5

Science title
How to Sparkle at Assessing Science	1 897675 20 8
How to Sparkle at Science Investigations	1 897675 36 4

If you would like further information on these or other titles published by Brilliant Publications, please write to the address given below.

Published by Brilliant Publications,
The Old School Yard, Leighton Road, Northall, Dunstable,
Bedfordshire LU6 2HA

Written by Jo Laurence
Illustrated by Kate Ford
Cover photograph by Martyn Chillmaid

Printed in Malta by Interprint Ltd

© Jo Laurence 1996
ISBN 1 897675 14 3

First published 1996
Reprinted 1998, 1999
10 9 8 7 6 5 4 3 2

The right of Jo Laurence to be identified as author of this work has been asserted by her in accordance with the Copyright, Designs and Patents Act 1988.

Pages 8-48 may be photocopied by individual teachers for class use, without permission from the publisher. The materials may not be reproduced in any other form or for any other purpose without the prior permission of the publisher.

Contents

	Page		*Page*
Introduction	4	How many words?	26
How to use this book	5	The answer rhymes!	27
Links to the National Curriculum	6	Rhyme riddles	28
Extension ideas	7	Solve the riddles	29
		Riddle-me-ree	30
Activities		Rhyming words	31
Which sound?	8	Goose or giant?	32
First sounds	9	Sounds like	33
Matching sounds	10	ch and sh	34
Last sounds	11	Finish the words	35
What's the sound?	12	Catch the rhyme	36
Matching ends	13	Shhhh… silent letters	37
Begin and end	14	Sounds like	38
In the middle	15	Which ones?	39
Which letter?	16	Which ones blend?	40
Short vowels	17	th in the middle	41
Long vowels	18	Say the sounds	42
Colour the vowels	19	Colour the kites	43
Fill in the long vowels	20	Riddle a word	44
Which blend?	21	What do you hear?	45
Blending middle	22	Ooooh …	46
More sounds	23	These words rhyme	47
Finish the word	24	I can rhyme	48
R for riddle	25		

Introduction

This book is one of a set of four devoted to basic strategies which will help early or beginning readers to find their way through the maze of complicated skills which make up the ability to read.

All the activities in this book are to do with learning sounds and using that knowledge to build words. It is widely recognised today that 'onset and rime' are very important skills for the early reader to acquire and this book focuses on beginning, medial and ending sounds, as well as on rhyme.

The objectives of a phonics programme are generally accepted to be:

- to develop knowledge of letter form and sound which will give the child a decoding strategy for unfamiliar words not apparent from context;

- to develop an ability to blend separate sounds to form words;

- to give the child insight into the nature of letters, how their sounds change in relation to other letters around them;

- to give lots of practice in listening and discriminating sounds;

- to give lots of practice in identifying and discriminating the visual forms of groups of letters;

- to help the children to recognise and identify familiar parts of new words;

- to demonstrate and teach the inconsistencies of English spelling.

Sounds and phonic rules need to be taught through the use of words and, wherever possible, words contained in a child's sight vocabulary and/or a child's own speech vocabulary. For example, quite obviously the word **dog** is more meaningful to a child than the symbols **d**, **o**, **g**. It is better to bring the child's attention to the sounds after he/she has learned the word. Letter sounds, of course, change according to their context (look for example at the **a** in **cat**, **water**, and **all**), therefore the use of whole words to demonstrate sounds is important.

In developing these sheets we were limited to using vocabulary which could be easily illustrated. However, with your input the sheets can be used as models and the activities developed to encompass a much larger range of words. Any sheet which is used in isolation should be followed with reading material with which the children may apply what they have learned or had reinforced from the sheets. In other words, make the learning functional as soon as possible.

The other three books in this series deal with the alphabet and alphabetical order, word recognition and prediction skills and the development of sequencing and comprehension skills.

How to use this book

The activities in this book are designed to supplement your chosen reading material.

They may be used with individual children or with small groups, as the need and opportunity arises. They have been clearly designed to have as little text as possible so that they are easily accessible to the beginning reader. In spite of this, some children may need you to read the page through carefully with them before they tackle the work.

In some cases it might be useful, as a reinforcement activity after they have been used as sheets, to cut the words from the pages and use them in a more kinaesthetic way. For instance, those pages where words or sounds need to be circled may be cut and the exercise extended by the children having to handle the words and letters and actually physically sort them out. In this way there can be the added value factor of having the children work in pairs or small groups to sort and match the material from several of the pages at one time. This activity will support and strengthen the original task.

The sheets should be used flexibly, not as a matter of course beginning at page 1 and working through the book. Not all children will need all the sheets. Knowledge of the children's individual needs and of the sheets will help you to provide a balanced and useful programme for each child.

Links to the National Curriculum

This book fits in with the National Curriculum Programme of Study for Key Stage 1 Reading attainment:

2 Key Skills

a   Pupils should be taught to read with fluency, accuracy, understanding and enjoyment, building on what they already know. In order to help them develop understanding of the nature and purpose of reading, they should be given an extensive introduction to books, stories and words in print around them. Pupils should be taught the alphabet, and be made aware of the sounds of spoken language in order to develop phonological awareness. They should also be taught to use various approaches to word identification and recognition, and to use their understanding of grammatical structure and the meaning of the text as a whole to make sense of print.

b   Within a balanced and coherent programme, pupils should be taught to use the following knowledge, understanding and skills.

Phonic knowledge, focusing on the relationships between print symbols and sound patterns. Opportunities should be given for:

- recognising alliteration, sound patterns and rhyme, and relating them to patterns in letters;

- considering syllables in longer words;

- identifying initial and final sounds in words;

- identifying and using a comprehensive range of letters and sounds, including combinations of letters, blends and digraphs, and paying specific attention to their use in the formation of words;

- recognising inconsistencies in phonic patterns;

- recognising some letters do not always produce a sound themselves but influence the sound of others.

Extension ideas

The following ideas will help to extend children's phonic skills:

- A game to play in small groups. Make a list of word families, eg **bell**, **tell**, **well**, **shell**, **sell**. Children stand. You call out words but try to trick them with a word that isn't in the same family, eg **ball**. They have to bounce down into sitting when they hear the wrong sound. You can begin this game with initial sounds and develop it from there.

- Children move, hop, skip or jump in a circle. The teacher calls 'Stop', chooses a child and calls a sound (beginning, ending, blend, vowel etc). Before the rest of the children can count to ten the child shouts another word with the same sound.

- Have the children all together. Play 'May I go?' One child is 'it'. This child calls (for example) 'I'm going to the moon'. The other children in turn say 'Can I go with you?' The reply is 'Yes, if you bring something beginning with **m**.' Likewise for 'going to town' something beginning with **t** etc.

- Make a set of sound cards, three cards for each sound you are trying to teach. Play with a small group of children, maximum four. Use no more than five sounds at a time. Place the cards on the table. Go round the children in turn. If you were teaching initial consonants such as **b**, **d**, **p**, you would say, 'find me the cards that start **b-ed, b-at, b-ad**'. The child with the most cards wins. Keep introducing new sounds.

- Have the children in two teams. Give Team A a word (for example 'sat') and Team B a word (for example, 'let'). The children in each team take it in turns to write on the board a word that rhymes with their word. They all sit down when the whole team has played. The team with the most correct words wins.

- Make up stories involving words that rhyme. You can tell the story but need to have the words already written on a board. The children have to decide which is the correct word. For example, you might say: 'Ben, the dog, wanted to go for a …' and show them 'walk' and 'talk'. Your next sentence might be: 'The dog got into a …' and your words might be 'night' and 'fight'. As the children get used to this game they will be able to help you make up the stories and supply the words.

- Teach the children the concept of syllables to help them absorb phonic knowledge. The easiest way to do this is to have them clap out the rhythms of their own and their peer's names.

- Working with a group, give the children words with the same initial blends, for example, '**shop, sheep, shed**'. Ask the children to tell you what the beginning sound is and have one of them write it down for the group. Ask for other words beginning with the same blend. To extend this activity ask for words ending with the blend and gradually move on to three-letter blends.

Which sound?

Circle the letter that you hear at the beginning of each name.

Can you write all the names?

1 _____ 6 _____
2 _____ 7 _____
3 _____ 8 _____
4 _____ 9 _____
5 _____

Colour the star if you can write the words.

First sounds

Circle the pictures in each row which begin with the sound of the letter.

l

t

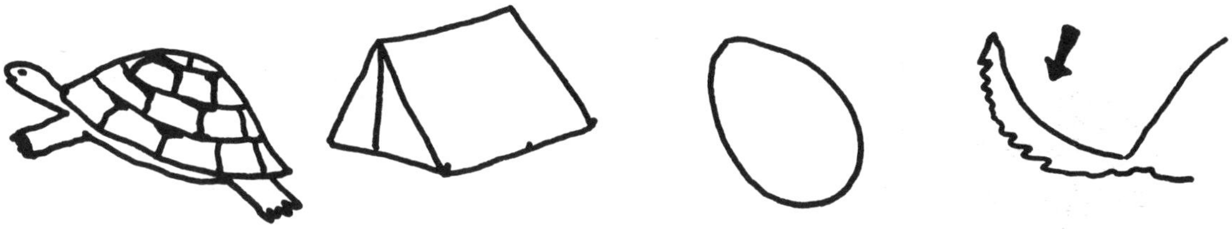

d

f

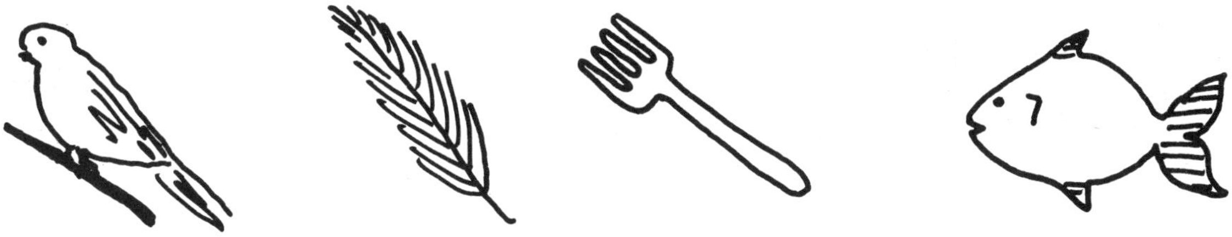

p

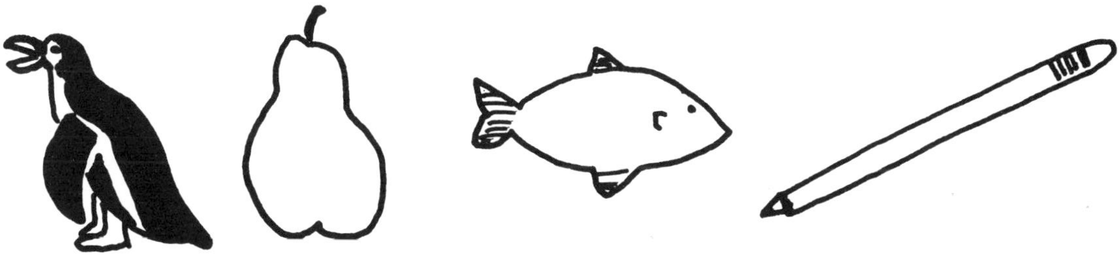

Colour the star if you can name all the things.

© Jo Laurence
This page may be photocopied for use in the classroom only.

How to Sparkle at Phonics

Matching sounds

Match the pictures to the letter that begins their name.

Write the words here if you can.

p _____   b _____
p _____   b _____
r _____   c _____
r _____   c _____
h _____   g _____
h _____   g _____

Colour the star if you can name all the things.

Last sounds

Circle the letter that ends each picture name.

Write the words here:

1 _____ 6 _____
2 _____ 7 _____
3 _____ 8 _____
4 _____ 9 _____
5 _____

Colour the star if you can name all the pictures.

What's the sound?

Write the letter for the ending sound.

cra__

doo__

fro__

fo__

brea__

crow__

foo__

dru__

bu__

Colour the star if you can draw and name something that ends with 't'.

Matching ends

Match the pictures with the letters that end their name.

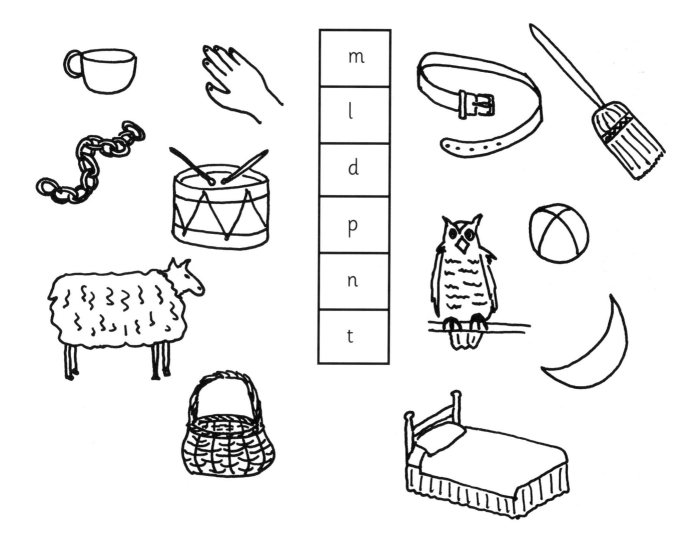

Write or draw six more words that end with:

m _____
l _____
d _____
p _____
n _____

Colour the star if you know a word that ends with 'g'.

Begin and end

Write the letters that begin and end each picture name.

1
__oo__

2
__i__

3
__a__

4
__oa__

5
__ee__

6
__o__

7
__i__

8
__a__

9
__u__

Write the names here:

1 _____   6 _____
2 _____   7 _____
3 _____   8 _____
4 _____   9 _____
5 _____

Colour the star if you can draw something that fits 't__y'.

How to Sparkle at Phonics

In the middle

Circle the letter you hear in the middle of each picture name.

Write the names here:

1 _____ 6 _____
2 _____ 7 _____
3 _____ 8 _____
4 _____ 9 _____
5 _____

Colour the star if you can draw or write a word with 'b' in the middle.

Which letter?

Write which sound you hear in the middle.

It is a _____.   It is a _____.   It is a _____.

It is a _____.   It is a _____.   It is a _____.

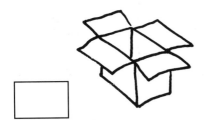   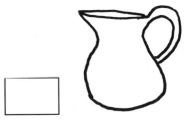

It is a _____.   It is a _____.   It is a _____.

Colour the star if you know what the letters a, e, i, o, u are called.

How to Sparkle at Phonics
16

Short vowels

These letters are called vowels. You can sometimes hear their sounds in the middle of words.

Trace the vowel sound in each word.

cat   nest   win

rock   tub

Put the short vowel sounds into these words. Say the words.

a	e	i	o	u
b_g	h_n	p_n	d_t	t_b
r_g	p_n	t_n	f_g	m_d
s_d	t_n	s_p	l_t	f_n
p_t	s_t	ch_p	st_p	b_n
l_p	l_t	f_g	ch_p	cl_b

Colour the star if you can read all the words.

Long vowels

Sometimes the vowels 'say their name'. When they do this they are called **LONG** vowels.

Say the sounds.

Trace the vowel sound in each word.

cage   feet   kite

rope   tube

Put the long vowel sounds into these words. Say the words.

a	e	i	o	u
b__ke	__ __l	t__e	sn__w	m__sic
st__y	f__ __l	f__ve	g__	c__be
m__ke	tr__ __	sl__ce	g__es	s__it
l__ke	ch__ __se	p__e	bl__w	r__le
s__y	wh__ __l	sl__de	t__e	p__pil

Colour the star if you can read all the words.

How to Sparkle at Phonics

Colour the vowels

If the word has a short vowel sound, colour the balloon red.
If the word has a long vowel sound, colour the balloon green.

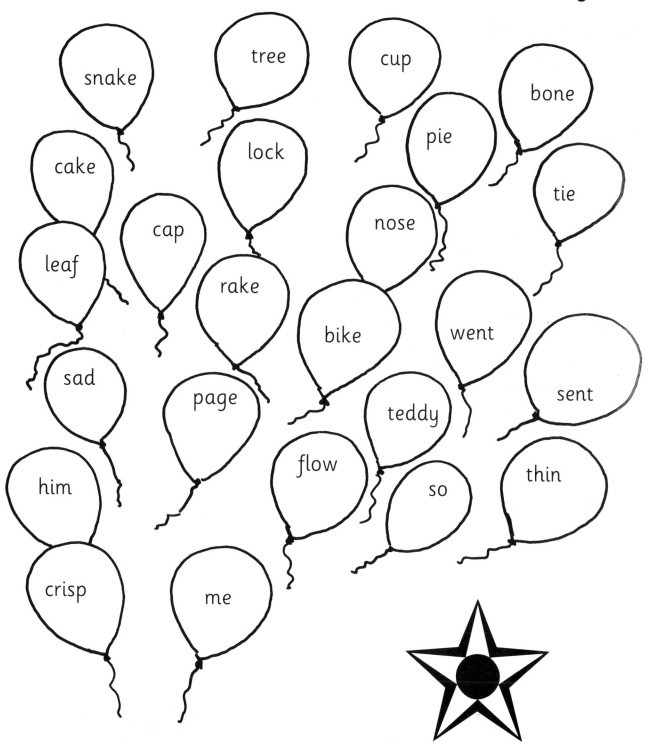

Colour the star if you can read all the words.

Fill in the long vowels

Write a, e, i, o or u in each word.
Draw a picture of what it is.

m__sic

c__ke

l__ke

f__ __t

n__se

b__ke

Colour the star if you can colour a
sentence about one of the words.

Sentence: _____

_____

_____

Which blend?

Circle the blend you hear at the beginning of each picture name. Say the sounds.

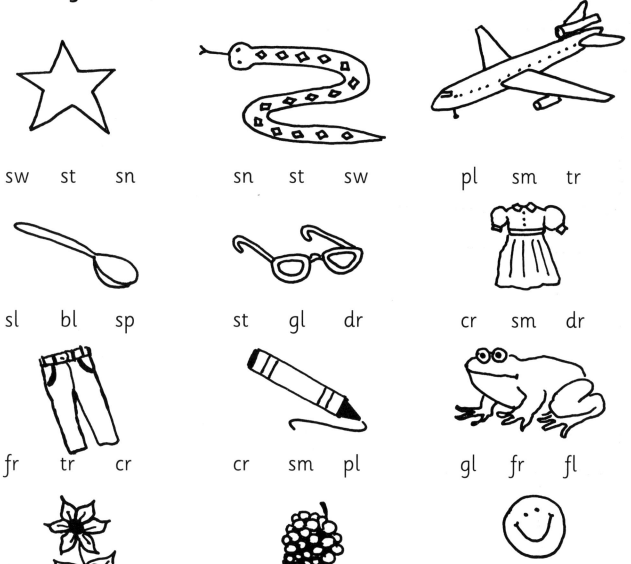

sw   st   sn   sn   st   sw   pl   sm   tr

sl   bl   sp   st   gl   dr   cr   sm   dr

fr   tr   cr   cr   sm   pl   gl   fr   fl

pl   fl   tr   st   br   gr   sm   st   tr

Colour the star if you can say all the sounds.

Blending riddle

Do you know these sounds?

Trace the sound at the beginning of each word. Match the words that rhyme.

where   shoe

shop   chin

chew   there

then   cheese

thin   chop

these   when

Write four words of your own.

sh _____

ch _____

th _____

wh _____

Colour the star if you can
say all the words.

More sounds

These sounds usually come at the ends of words.

ld   nt   nd

Read the words and write the sound at the end of each one in the box.

friend ☐   end ☐

plant ☐   hold ☐

went ☐   front ☐

old ☐   find ☐

band ☐   cold ☐

paint ☐   want ☐

Write two words ending with 'ld':
_____
_____

Write two words ending with 'nt':
_____
_____

Write two words ending with 'nd':
_____
_____

Colour the star if you have made six words of your own.

Finish the word

These sounds often come at the ends of words.

Write one of the endings for each word. The shapes will help you.

1    7

2 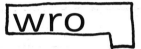   8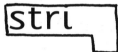

3   9

4 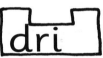   10

5 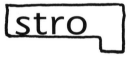   11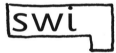

6    12

Write the words here:

1 _____   7 _____
2 _____   8 _____
3 _____   9 _____
4 _____   10 _____
5 _____   11 _____
6 _____   12 _____

Colour the star if you can write the words.

How to Sparkle at Phonics

R for riddle

Each of these words has an 'r' after a vowel. The 'r' makes the vowel sound different. Write the words in the boxes.

You can drive it

It flies and eats worms

It can gallop

A child that's not a boy

There's one on this page

You might get one in the post

Cat and dogs have it

Ships sail to it

A kind of tree with needles

Farmers grow it

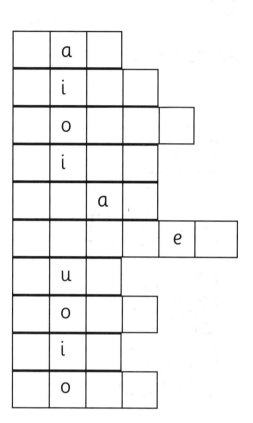

Can you name these things that have an 'r' after a vowel?

_____ _____

Colour the star if you can make up a riddle for your new words.

© Jo Laurence
This page may be photocopied for use in the classroom only.

How to Sparkle at Phonics

How many words?

Solve the puzzle. All the missing words have 'ou' in them.

1   We live in a h__ __ __ __.
2   There are cl__ __ __ __ in the sky.
3   A m__ __ __ __ is very small and furry.
4   There are a hundred pennies in a p__ __ __ __.
5   A sign will show you the way __ __t.

Draw a picture for each sentence and label with the word.

Colour the star if you know which clue means 'exit'.

The answer rhymes!

Find the missing word. It begins with the letter 'd' and rhymes with the word in the oval.

One end of the swimming pool is d_____ . (keep)

We d_____ in the snow with a spade. (big)

The sun shines all d_____ in the summer. (lay)

I d_____ the table every week. (just)

We go up and d_____ the road on our bikes. (brown)

When night falls it gets d_____ . (bark)

Can you find another word to rhyme with these words? (Tip: use any letter to begin.)

play   keep   big

just   brown   lay

sheep   wig   bark

Colour the star if you can make up a rhyme riddle of your own.

© Jo Laurence
This page may be photocopied for use in the classroom only.

Rhyme riddles

Find the missing word. It begins with the letter 'r' and rhymes with the word in the cloud.

1 Some holes are square, some are r_____ .   *found*
2 Chicken and r_____ are good for dinner.   *mice*
3 Green means go, r_____ means stop.   *bed*
4 After running you need a r_____ .   *best*
5 You might win the r_____ .   *face*
6 If you don't like running you could r_____ your bike.   *hide*

Can you find another word to rhyme with these words? (Tip: use any letter to begin.)

Colour the star if you can say six words that rhyme with 'rat'.

Solve the riddles

All of the answers begin with 'p' and rhyme with the word in the box.

1 I am a kind of fruit.
   I have a soft skin.
   I rhyme with reach .
   I am a p_____ .

2 I am a small vegetable.
   I am green and round.
   I rhyme with sea .
   I am a p_____ .

3 I am an animal's foot.
   A cat has four of me.
   I rhyme with saw .
   I am a p_____ .

4 I am a kind of bucket.
   I carry water.
   I rhyme with sail .
   I am a p_____ .

Match the words that rhyme.

sea	big
hole	tail
reach	bee
dig	mole
sail	teach

Colour the star if you can say six words that rhyme with 'sea'.

Riddle-me-ree

All of the answers begin with 'h' and rhyme with the word in the cloud.

1. I am something to do in a game.
   When you do it, someone has to look or seek.
   I rhyme with {wide}
   I am h_____ .

2. I can be dug in the sand.
   You can put something in me.
   I rhyme with {foal.}
   I am h_____ .

3. You might need a hook to do me.
   You can do me to your coat.
   I rhyme with {sang.}
   I am h_____ .

4. I am on a car.
   You can toot me.
   I rhyme with {born.}
   I am a h_____ .

Match the words that rhyme.

born	tried
cheer	torn
foal	fear
pot	bowl
wide	dot

Colour the star if you can say all these words.

Rhyming words

Find the rhyming words.

key rhymes with ⬜

kitten rhymes with ⬜

kite rhymes with ⬜

jam rhymes with ⬜

joke rhymes with ⬜

join rhymes with ⬜

zero rhymes with ⬜

zip rhymes with ⬜

Colour the star is you can write and draw something that rhymes with 'wagon'.

The word is: _____

Goose or giant?

The letter 'g' makes two different sounds.

One is 'g' as in <u>goose</u> or <u>game</u>.
We call this 'hard g'.

One is 'g' as in <u>giant</u> or <u>gem</u>.
We call this 'soft g'.

Name these things beginning with a 'hard g'.

g_____   g_____   g_____

Name these things beginning with a 'soft g'.

g_____   g_____   g_____

Colour the star if you can say a name beginning with a 'soft G' and a name beginning with a 'hard G'.

Sounds like

Sometimes the letter 'c' sounds like 'k' as in:

comb   cup   cone

Sometimes the letter 'c' sounds like 's' as in:

cereal   juice   bicycle

Draw a line from the 'c' word to the sound it makes.

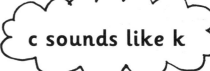

code

circle

calf

candle

Cinderella

case

cost

circus   centre

curl

Can you name these 'c' words?

c_____   c_____   __c__ c_____

Colour the star if you can read all the 'c' words on this page.

© Jo Laurence
This page may be photocopied for use in the classroom only.

How to Sparkle at Phonics
33

ch and sh

Say the name of each thing. If it begins with the sound 'ch' colour it yellow. If it begins with the sound 'sh' colour it blue.

How many 'sh' words? ☐

How many 'ch' words? ☐

Write the words:

1 _____
2 _____
3 _____
4 _____
5 _____
6 _____
7 _____
8 _____

Colour the star if you can name two more 'sh' words and two more 'ch' words.

Finish the words

All of these words have 'sh' or 'ch' in them, sometimes at the beginning, sometimes at the end. Read the words. Fill in the spaces.

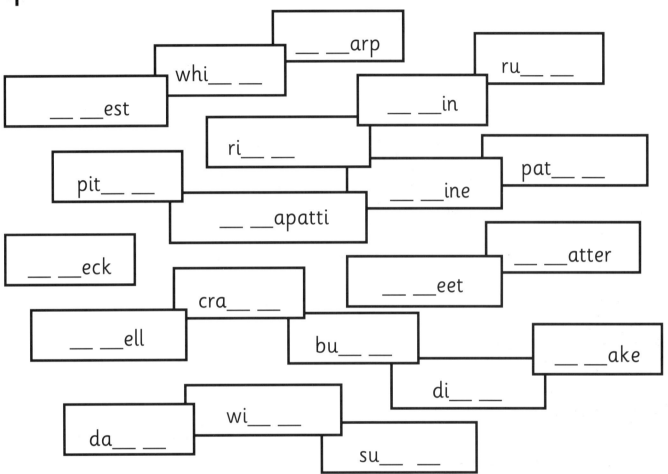

Use these words:

which	chest	rich
rush	shine	such
chapatti	chin	dash
patch	chatter	sheet
check	shell	wish
sharp	shake	dish
bush	crash	pitch

Colour the star if you can read all the words.

Catch the rhyme

Say the words. Draw a balloon for the word that rhymes in each group.

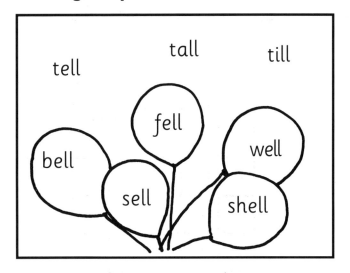

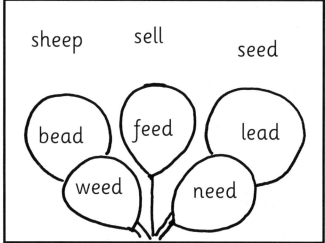

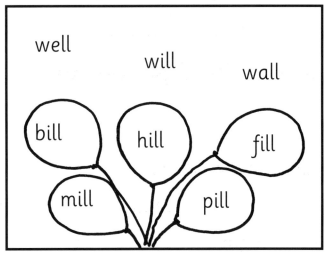

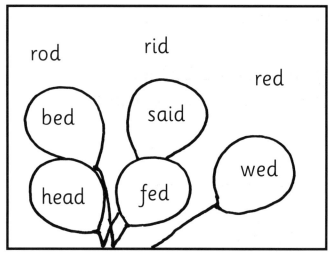

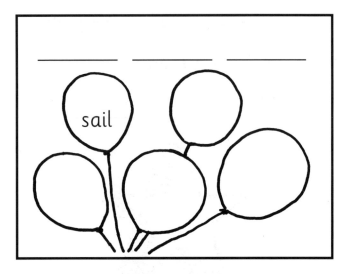

Colour the star if you can think of a set of word balloons of your own for words that rhyme with 'sail'.

Shhhhh ... silent letters

Sometimes letters are silent.

If 'k' comes before 'n' you can't hear it. See if you can do these 'silent k' puzzles.

1 You use this to cut.
2 You tie this.
3 You do this with your fist on a door.
4 You have two of these.
5 You can make clothes by doing this.
6 You learn so that you _____.

k	n			
k	n			
k	n				
k	n			
k	n			
k	n			

If 'w' comes before 'r' you can't hear it. See if you can do these 'silent w' puzzles.

w	r		
w	r			
w	r			
w	r			
w	r		
w	r			

1 A kind of small bird.
2 Just above your hand.
3 It's not right.
4 You do this with a pen or pencil.
5 You do this to presents.
6 A ship at the bottom of the sea.

Colour the star if you can say any more silent letter words.

Sounds like

Some of these things begin with the sound 'cr' and some begin with the sound 'tr'. Join them to the sound that is right for them.

Can you write the words?

'cr' words		'tr' words	
1 _____	4 _____	1 _____	4 _____
2 _____	5 _____	2 _____	5 _____
3 _____	6 _____	3 _____	6 _____

Colour the star if you can write all the words.

Which ones?

Say these sounds:

Circle the pictures in each row that begin with the sound.

pl				
bl				
fl				
cl				
sl				

Colour the star if you can say all the names.

Which ones blend?

Say these sounds:

Circle the pictures in each row that begin with the sound.

br	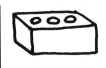			
dr				
fr				
gr				
pr				

Colour the star if you can say all the names.

th in the middle

When 'th' comes in the middle of a word it sounds like 'th' in <u>there</u> and <u>this</u>. Say these words. Listen for the sound 'th' makes.

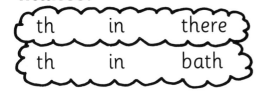
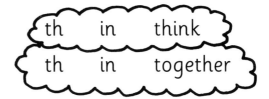

Which two sound the same?

Do the puzzle.

1 This man has a child.
2 This woman has a child.
3 This boy has a sister.
4 Shoes are made from this.
5 Birds' wings are made of these.

Write six 'th' words here.

th at the beginning	th in the middle	th at the end
1 _____	3 _____	5 _____
2 _____	4 _____	6 _____

Colour the star if you can find six words with 'th' in your reading book.

Say the sounds

Say the sounds:

Circle the pictures in each row that begin with the sound.

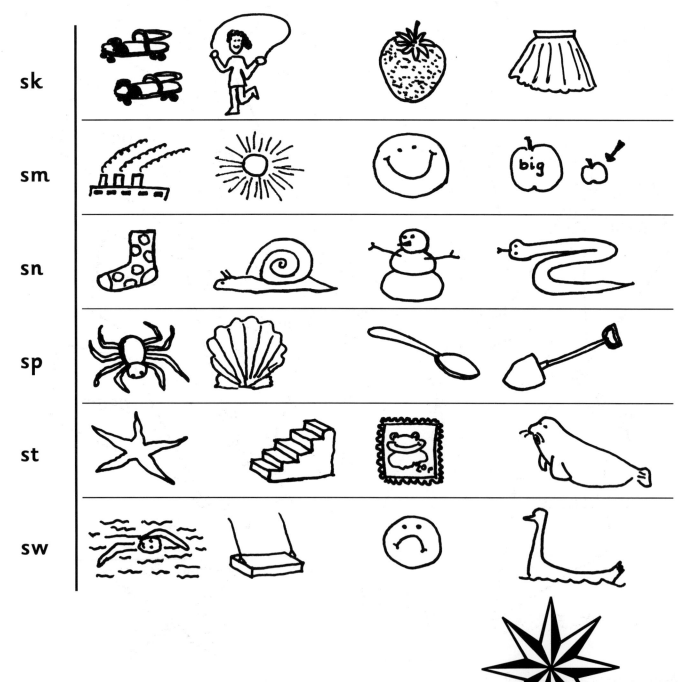

Colour the star if you know three more 'sp' words.

Colour the kites

Sometimes 'ea' makes a sound as in <u>tea</u>. Colour all these kites red.

Sometimes 'ea' makes a sound as in <u>head</u>. Colour all these kites blue.

- leaf
- tea
- seal
- feather
- spread
- beach
- head
- bead
- meat
- bread
- leather
- bean
- peach
- beat
- heather

How many reds? ☐

How many blues? ☐

Colour the star if you know another way to write the red sound.

© Jo Laurence
This page may be photocopied for use in the classroom only.

How to Sparkle at Phonics

Riddle a word

Find the 'oi' words and write them in the flowers.

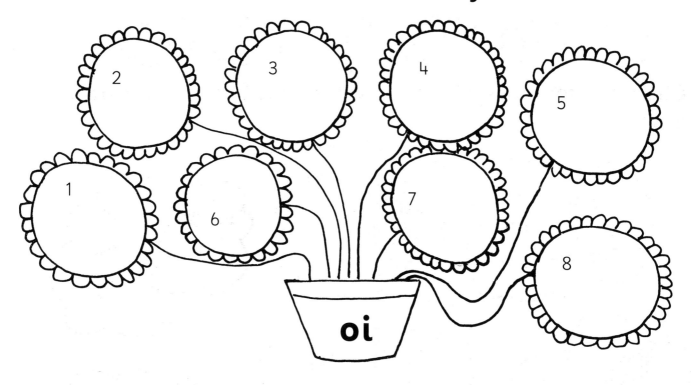

1   You put seeds and plants into this (__oi__).
2   You talk with this (__oi__ __).
3   You need this at the end of your pencil to write (__oi__ __).
4   Money made of metal (__oi__).
5   This can be loud or quiet (__oi__ __).
6   You cook chips in this (oi__).
7   A kind of spring (__oi__).
8   The water in the kettle does this (__oi__).

Colour the star if you know another way
of writing an 'oi' sound.
Clue: think of something you play with.

How to Sparkle at Phonics

What do you hear?

Read these sounds:

Circle the sound you hear in each name. Some might trick you!

Write the names.

1 _____   5 _____
2 _____   6 _____
3 _____   7 _____
4 _____   8 _____

Colour the star if you can find words with each of these sounds in your reading book.

Ooooh ...

The letters 'oo' make two sounds.

Short 'oo' says 'oo' as in <u>book</u>.

Long 'oo' says 'oo' as in <u>moon</u>.

Put the words in the right box.

short oo

long oo

hook, moon, brook, book, soon, tooth, boom, shook, room, look, boot, brook, spoon, took, crook, boo hoo

Colour the star if you can draw a moon.

These words rhyme

Find a word to rhyme with each one.

	My word is		My word is
drive	_____	prize	_____
bond	_____	train	_____
care	_____	skip	_____
spots	_____	self	_____
elf	_____	toad	_____
smell	_____	when	_____
grass	_____	ox	_____
hand	_____	yellow	_____
indoors	_____	zero	_____
grapes	_____		
scurry	_____		
lend	_____		
claw	_____		
never	_____		

Colour the star if you can read all the words.

© Jo Laurence
This page may be photocopied for use in the classroom only.

I can rhyme

How many words can you find to rhyme with each of these words?

blue _____ _____ _____

air _____ _____ _____

fly _____ _____ _____

jet _____ _____ _____

kick _____ _____ _____

three _____ _____ _____

bread _____ _____ _____

snow _____ _____ _____

play _____ _____ _____

rest _____ _____ _____

moat _____ _____ _____

Colour the star if you can read all the words.

How to Sparkle at Phonics
© Jo Laurence
This page may be photocopied for use in the classroom only.